FAMILY TREE

MW01491205

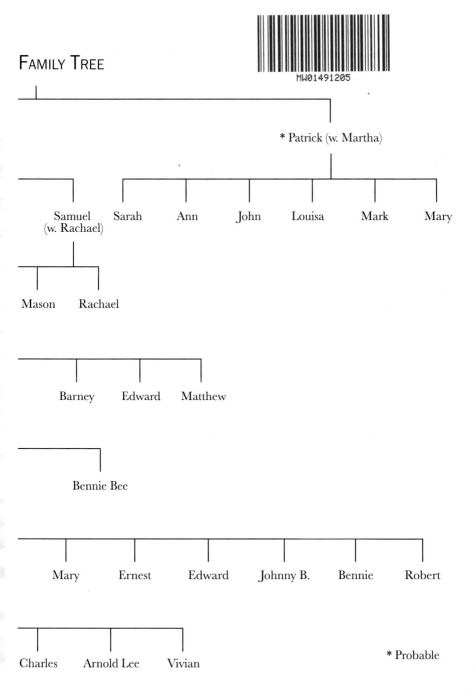

* Patrick (w. Martha)

Samuel (w. Rachael) Sarah Ann John Louisa Mark Mary

Mason Rachael

Barney Edward Matthew

Bennie Bee

Mary Ernest Edward Johnny B. Bennie Robert

Charles Arnold Lee Vivian

* Probable

SPARTANBURG COUNTY
PUBLIC LIBRARIES

Trotting Sally

THE ROOTS AND LEGACY OF A FOLK HERO

Trotting Sally

THE ROOTS AND LEGACY OF A FOLK HERO

By John Thomas Fowler

KENNEDY
FREE PRESS

Kennedy Free Press
Spartanburg County Public Libraries

First printing: January 2014
Cover designs: Miranda Mims Sawyer
Interior design: JoAnn Mitchell Brasington
Printed in Spartanburg, S.C., by Southeastern Printing Inc.

KENNEDY
FREE PRESS

Spartanburg County Public Libraries
151 South Church Street
Spartanburg, S.C. 29306
www.infodepot.org

Front cover photograph courtesy of the Herald-Journal Willis Collection,
Spartanburg County Public Libraries
Back cover photograph by LeighAnn Snuggs
Clip art courtesy of FCIT
Kennedy Free Press editor: Susan Thoms

I dedicate this book to all the unsung street
and medicine-show performers, fiddle and banjo players
and old-time musicians who have inspired,
and who continue to inspire, many generations.

ACKNOWLEDGMENTS

In the fall of 1987, I stumbled upon a wonderful newspaper article written by Inman Times staff reporter Hilda Morrow. It told of a charismatic upcountry man nicknamed Trotting Sally who lived around the turn of the 20th century. The article included a photo of him holding his fiddle. I was immediately captivated. It was almost like I was reading about a legendary character in a make-believe story. Could it really be possible that a folk hero of this magnitude had lived here in the upcountry of South Carolina? This is when my research began. Over the years I have been able to splice together genealogical facts, historical information and great storytelling dating back to 1790. The task of researching family history can be overwhelming. I researched newsprint stories, slave schedules, maps, death certificates, census records, court documents and a mountain of other material. The more I discovered, the more I knew his story had to be told. Sometimes I felt like George "Trotting Sally" Mullins was encouraging me along the way. I've been lucky to have resources, support and assistance from a number of friends and colleagues. Many new friendships have been made throughout this project, but possibly the most treasured is that of Alfred Mullins, Trotting Sally's great-grandson. We have spent hours together laughing, sharing stories and information and visiting the lands of his ancestors. He is such an inspiration to me.

Many thanks to William Austin, who is a direct descendant of the historic Austin family of Greenville County, South Carolina. I very much enjoyed the afternoon I spent under the majestic oaks at Gilder plantation chatting with him about local history and family lore.

The rare newspaper article from Pacolet, South Carolina, that my good friend Bob Owens shared with me, which had belonged to his father, was a gold mine of information. For this, I thank Bob Owens and the late Leroy Owens.

I also want to express my gratitude to amateur genealogists Betty Jean Dill and the late Lynn Hicks Sellers. They led me to a number of finds that I simply would not have discovered.

To Mary Ann Dempster, a special thank-you for her first-round editing and for being the encouraging spirit I needed to do this project right.

I wish to express my sincere appreciation to Susan Thoms, local history and genealogy researcher and Kennedy Free Press editor at the Spartanburg County Headquarters Library. Without her knowledge, guidance and interest in this project, it would not have been possible. Thank you for challenging my research to insure no stone was left unturned.

LeighAnn Snuggs has played an important role in helping me see this project through. Her endless devotion, passion, skill, and support given to me and this project are beyond measure. There are no words to express my sincere gratitude.

There are countless others who have been instrumental in helping in the collection of facts for this story. I thank everyone that has contributed.

I am proud to share the information I've been able to collect all because of a captivating article I read years ago and hope this book, the legaćy of Trotting Sally, serves as an inspiration for others that come after me.

John Thomas Fowler

September 29, 2013

iv

PROLOGUE

Born into slavery on a plantation in Greenville District, South Carolina, in 1856, his name was simply George. As a boy, after emancipation, he and his family migrated to Spartanburg County to live on property where his father was raised. This property, once known as the Mullins plantation, became his namesake. As an adult, George, a husband and father, worked as a sharecropper and farmhand. Although he primarily earned his living as a laborer, his legacy is that of a charismatic street musician and showman.

Known as "Trotting Sally" by most, George Washington Mullins[*] enjoyed entertaining. During his street shows he would caper about while playing his fiddle, which he claimed he made and named Rosalie. His audiences no doubt wondered why he trotted and leapt about and how he produced such sounds with Rosalie. What is without doubt is that George was captivating and had a never-ending energy and spirit.

As an African American living in the Jim Crow South, George enjoyed a certain notoriety few persons of color experienced. There were a number of newspaper articles written about him, most notably a 1907 New York Times piece that claimed his

---

[*] As with many surnames of this time period, Mullin/Mullen/Mullins/Mullens had alternate spellings. For clarity sake and because it is the spelling the descendants ultimately chose to use, Mullins will be used here.

nickname was given to him when he was young after he raced a horse to town. In 1923, a Spartanburg store used Trotting Sally and his reputation in a newspaper ad to entice shoppers. African-American portraits by noted Spartanburg photographer Alfred T. Willis were rare, and George's is the most notable. Even his obituary, which appeared in the Spartanburg Herald, read like a column celebrating his life. Other stories continued to surface in newsprint years after his death.

George enjoyed his fame throughout many communities in the upcountry of South Carolina and in western North Carolina. Some say he seemed to be mentally challenged because of his socially awkward behavior and unusual character traits. Some were afraid of him, while others made light or laughed and jeered. Yet he also seemed to possess a keen sense of street smarts, calculating his whereabouts, even using someone to collect his earnings from busking. This leads some to believe that he was just putting on an act, which begs the question: Was performing on the streets easier than picking cotton in the hot sun? After all, like many African Americans at the turn of the 20th century, Mullins had no education or technical job skills, leaving him with little promise for a better life. Perhaps his character and talents simply were misunderstood as he struggled to survive in a racially segregated society.

George's true character remains difficult to pin down. In many ways he was a contradiction — a married man who claimed to be widowed, an African American who achieved local press during a national epidemic of lynching. Perhaps, like John Henry and Johnny Appleseed, Mullins is an American folk hero — a true representation of South Carolina heritage, history and culture.

.

1

Trotting Sally was born into slavery on a cotton plantation in the upcountry of South Carolina in 1856. He was the property of Dr. Thomas Collins Austin, a prominent Greenville physician and planter. His birth name was George.

George's maternal grandmother, Mason, was born in 1794. As a young woman, she served as a domestic slave to John James, a well-to-do planter from Spartanburg. Mason may have been the daughter of one of the James family's female slaves or may have been purchased or received as a gift.

John was originally from Amelia County, Virginia, and was born on December 29, 1777. His father, Thomas James Jr., was a soldier in the Revolutionary War. Thomas was killed in 1779 at the Battle of Stono Ferry near Charleston, South Carolina, according to family history. John's mother, Mary Ann Jones James, later married William "Major Billy" Foster, who also had served in the war. They settled in the Beech Springs area of Spartanburg County.

Beech Springs, which was named for the abundance of beech trees that grow along the waters of the Tyger River, is located west of the city of Spartanburg. White people began settling the area as early as 1760 near the present-day towns of Wellford, Duncan, Lyman and Fairforest.

When John came of age he returned to Virginia for a brief time, likely to claim property that was given to him after the death of his father. He sold the land and returned to Beech Springs. With his mother and stepfather's blessings, he purchased property near the present-day vicinity of Mount Zion, Fort Prince and Falling Creek roads and Interstate 85.

The property, somewhat hilly with rich bottom land, consists of sandy red clay with clusters of sandstone — an excellent combination for growing crops such as short-staple cotton and for grazing livestock. Just where the James farmhouse was located is unknown — possibly near a water source. Likely the house was a two-story, wood-framed dwelling with three or four bedrooms, a sitting room or parlor and a dining room. The kitchen would have been located in the back detached from the main house. Outbuildings such as barns, sheds, a corn crib, spring house and slave quarters would have been close by.

In 1805, John married 18-year-old Jane Anderson Turner, who was born in Clark County, Georgia. Her parents were originally from Virginia. She likely had been visiting relatives in Beech Springs when she and John were introduced. Jane was the grandniece of John's stepfather, Major Billy.

In 1806, Jane gave birth to their only child, Mary "Polly" Turner James. Polly's primary caregiver may have been Mason, one of John's young domestic slaves. If so, Mason's responsibilities as nanny would have been numerous. Another female slave also worked in the James household as a domestic servant. She was three years younger than Mason. Her name was Rachael.

2

By the early 1820s, John had made his mark. He owned about 650 acres on which he raised livestock and planted cotton, corn and grain. He had a cotton gin, several barns, slave housing and a smokehouse. Land and slaves were the means for economic success, which gave him political clout and status within the community. While many farmers in the region were very poor, John was part of a growing community of well-to-do planters from the upcountry.

The year of 1823 began with promise for the James family. Polly was engaged to be married to Dr. Thomas Collins Austin of the Rocky Creek area of Greenville District. The Austins were successful planters with social and political influence. Common to the period, it is possible that this was an arranged marriage.

The Austins were one of the first white families to settle in Greenville County. Thomas's grandfather was Nathaniel Austin Sr., born in York, England, in 1720. He and his young family came to Virginia in 1750. His wife died in 1753, shortly after giving birth to their fifth son. Nathaniel then married Agnes Dickinson. They moved south in the 1760s to Little River Branch, which was a tributary of the Saluda River. It later was renamed Gilder Creek and runs through an unincorporated area of present-day Simpsonville. There Nathaniel built a residence he named Gilder. He and Agnes had six children, which brought the blended family to a total of 10 males and one female, Mary. Young Mary was murdered by Indians while coming home from a quilting party. Years later her brother, William, avenged her death by killing her murderers.

William was born in 1759 in Lunenburg County, Virginia. According to family history, he served under General Andrew Pickens during the Revolutionary War and fought at Musgrove Mill and Cowpens. He married Jane Collins of York, Pennsylvania, in 1783. They built a house near Gilder. Some referred to it as Gilder II. They had five children.

Thomas was born in 1790. He was extremely bright. As a youngster he walked "four muddy miles" to the county post office to get his copy of Benjamin Franklin's newspaper, the Pennsylvania Gazette (later published as the Saturday Evening Post). He enjoyed reading firsthand accounts of Napoleon's campaigns. He was privately schooled at home and after nine years was sent to South Carolina College in Columbia to enter his senior year. Young Thomas returned home after he learned he already had covered all the subjects needed.

William commanded and probably raised a regiment during the War of 1812. Thomas served as its paymaster. After the war, Thomas attended the Medical University of Pennsylvania.

Towering at 6'4", Thomas was striking in appearance and personality. He had steel blue eyes that flashed with a quick glance, a long straight nose and high cheekbones. His manners were austere and courtly. He could be as gentle as a child but in anger, his wrath was terrible. He was fondly called "Long Tom" due to his superb physique, erect posture and disciplined personality. He considered himself a meticulous Southern gentleman — he never crossed his legs, sat straight and erect in his chair, knees together and feet flat on the floor. He had a loud, booming voice that could be heard across the countryside. Family lore says he would stand on the front porch of his house and shout out orders to his slave and overseer, Cato, more than a mile way.

Polly and Thomas were wed on February 28, 1823, and that year Thomas built a plantation house they called Oakland. It is about a mile from Gilder and shares many of its features.

On March 15, mere weeks after the wedding, joy turned to tragedy when Polly's father died. John James was 45 years old. His death affected not only the family, but their slaves as well.

John's will, written in 1817, left his entire estate to his wife and child. Polly was given half of the estate, but no land. John wrote, "The remaining half of my estate I dispose of in the following manner viz, one Negro woman by the name of Rachael, and an other [sic] by the name of Mason, with all their increase, I give to my beloved Wife Jane James to be freely possessed and enjoyed by her, the said Jane James her and her heirs forever."

Of John's 30 slaves, Rachael and Mason were the only two mentioned by name. In contrast, the other slaves were listed in the will as "Land Negroes," likely field hands.

Dr. Austin, Jane's son-in-law, served as co-administrator and played a major role in coordinating the settlement of the large estate. In order to pay creditors, the estate administrators arranged the sale of some of John's assets, including the field slaves. They were appraised at $6,690.

Jane retained possession of the property as well as the livestock, household furnishings and field hands, along with Mason, Rachael and their children. Between 1816 and 1823, Mason had given birth to five children. The only known birth by Mason after John's death is that of a son, Samuel, who was not born until 1827. This may suggest that Mason's mate was sold in this transaction.

Jane appears to have spent several years mourning John's passing with bouts of depression and uncertainty. Her life was in shambles. Others were in control of the plantation and her future. Austin managed his mother-in-law's property. He may have farmed some of the land but likely leased or bargained for goods and services with other local farmers for the use of the land. Jane was looked after by family and close friends, including her second cousin, Phebe George Foster.

In 1824, Phebe's mother and Jane's cousin, Celia Foster, discussed Jane's health in a letter sent via Austin.

South Carolina Greenville District, 12th February 1824
Very Dear and affectionate Daughter —

We received your letter handed by Doctor Austin which gave us great satisfaction to hear that you were enjoying good health & that you were very well satisfied at the place you are, but sorry to hear that cousin Jane James still remain[s] in a very low state of health. Myself & family through mercy are enjoying a good degree of health for which we ought to be thankful. Your Uncle Moore's family are at present in pretty good health & sends their best love & respects to you. Your sisters and the family in general express a great anxiety to see you

& think the time long in your absent. Your grandfather often speaks of you as wishing to see you very much. Dear daughter I should have wrote to you by the post last week. But I went to the village the day I intended to write & was belated so that when I returned I had not the opportunity. I wish you to write by every convenient opportunity. There has nothing of importance occurred in the settlement that I know of since I saw you. Myself & family in general send our best love & respects to Cousin Jane James. Give my respect to all that may think worth while to inquire about me. There many things that I could write though nothing at present of great importance. I shall come to a close by describing myself most loving & affectionate mother until death.

— Celia Foster

N.B. I have sent you a piece of cambrick for a handkerchief. Some yarn for stockings & some peas for Cousin Jane James.

By the late 1820s, Austin was much more involved in the everyday operations at the James farm. He decided what to plant, when to harvest and what tools and animals to buy. Jane was completely powerless. Austin used her 16 slaves as he saw fit. He grew cotton as well as other crops and raised livestock. Thomas and Polly expected Jane to live out the rest of her days as a widow and to leave her property to them.

Jane, however, had other ideas. On September 5, 1829, she married Daniel C. Mullins. Just how and when Daniel and Jane met is unclear. He may have been hired as an overseer on Jane's farm or just been passing through. It does appear that he was new to the area. Daniel was British and may have been connected to one of the five Mullins families that settled in South Carolina around 1800. Maritime documents show a Daniel Mullins who traveled from Great Britain to Charleston in 1798. However, a direct connection cannot be established as these records are inconclusive.

It does appear that Daniel and Jane married at the spur of the moment, catching Thomas and Polly off guard. By law, administrative rights to Jane's property, including her slaves, would belong to her new husband and no longer be under Austin's control. Records suggest that when they were married Austin took "great offence" and quickly had Daniel indicted in Spartanburg for polygamy. No information was provided in the case on any other alleged wives. Jane responded in court, "As the said Daniel Mullen was a foreigner and stranger, many persons were induced to believe the truth to the charges."

While in jail awaiting trial, Mullins was sued in three separate cases for assumption of damages. These lawsuits appear not to have been directly related to Austin's allegations but still may have been influenced by him. It is also a possibility that individuals to whom Mullins was in debt saw in his marriage an opportunity to be paid. Mullins lost in each of the three cases and was ordered to pay damages totaling $900. It was his wife's money that likely settled these charges.

Daniel and Jane must have known that Austin would not easily relinquish his hold on the former James estate. Shortly after their marriage, Daniel granted his administrative rights to Jane's estate to a neighbor, Herbert Hawkins. This was no doubt a way of protecting Jane's property from lawsuits, but it did not stop Austin from making a claim on behalf of his wife's interest in her mother's property.

Just months prior to a jury finding Mullins innocent of the polygamy charge, Austin obtained a writ of ne exeat against both Jane and Daniel, which restrained them from selling any property. Austin then offered to drop all legal proceedings against Daniel if Jane would agree to purchase her daughter's portion of the estate.

The pressure worked. Jane and Daniel agreed to pay $3,000 plus interest and cost to Austin by five payment notes and the mortgage of their house, farm buildings and equipment, tools, livestock and all 16 slaves, including Mason and Rachael. Two days later, the Austins sold the real estate back to Jane and Daniel for $3,200. However, Thomas and Polly took all of the remaining assets, including six of the slaves and the household furnishings. Jane had only the real estate, Mason, Rachael and their children — ultimately leaving her with less than her late husband's will intended.

Perhaps the most important documentation in these proceedings is that Daniel's deed of administrative conveyance to neighbor Hawkins references Mason, Rachael and their children.

Mason's family was recorded as:
Mason, 35 years old
Ned, 14
Ellin, 12
Selvo, 11
Bob, 8
Dick, 7
Samuel, 18 months

Rachael's family was recorded as:
Rachael, 32 years old
Mary, 16
Sally, 15

Mason and Rachael may have been siblings, based on their close ages and relationship. Five of the slaves taken by the Austins — Cary, Kiza, Susan, Tom and Suba — appear not to be related to either Rachael or Mason. It is possible that the sixth, Patrick, was a sibling to the two women. Patrick was some five years younger than Rachael, chose the surname Mullins after emancipation and moved after the war to Campobello. This community also was to become home to relatives of George's in later years. If Patrick was a blood relative, his appearance in the 1870 census leaves a tantalizing clue: His birthplace was listed as Virginia. Perhaps his parents were original James slaves from Amelia County.

3

Austin's public attacks on Daniel and Jane no doubt affected their standing in society. Daniel never became a prominent member of the community. He does not appear to have been a member of any local church or social society, held no political office and never was called on to witness deeds or act as trustee.

Daniel's role as an outsider may have been part of his charm to Jane. As a widow, she had limited control over her assets and legal matters. Remarrying would simplify legal obstacles, yet marrying a man of prominence and power could have put her under the thumb of another man intent on controlling her. Not discounting love as the primary reason, marrying Daniel very likely was in Jane's best interest.

Despite the friction between the Mullins and Austin families, Polly remained Jane's sole heir if Daniel died before his wife. Between 1830 and 1840, though, that may have changed. The 1840 census lists two young white females in the Mullins household – one older than 10 and one younger. However, the age of the older child may have been overstated because the 1830 census lists no children in the household. This is the only documentation found to support the existence of these girls. By 1850, they have disappeared. What happened to them and whether they were the daughters of Jane and Daniel remains a mystery.

Daniel continued to be plagued by criminal and civil cases that ranged from assault and battery to trespassing. Though he was acquitted of all criminal charges, civil accusations continued to create a financial burden for the couple. They worked hard to recoup from their legal and financial losses. Even with the best of management skills, it is unlikely that they farmed all of their property. They simply did not have the manpower. Jane's role may have been keeping the books, paying creditors and helping to make business decisions, while Daniel likely oversaw farming responsibilities.

In 1839, three events that seem to be connected took place.

In July, Daniel and Jane traveled to Cannon County, Tennessee, and renewed their wedding vows. This provided legal documentation of their union since Tennessee recorded marriages and South Carolina did not. William Foster acted as the justice of the peace and may have been kin to the Spartanburg Fosters to whom both Jane and her late husband, John, were related.

Four months later, Daniel and Jane sold nearly half of their land to local investor and farmer Harvey Finch. Both Daniel and Jane signed the deed. Though Thomas and Polly probably weren't happy about it, they had no legal grounds to stop it. Daniel and Jane likely documented their union to deflect any possible questions about the legality of Daniel's role in the sale of the property. The 308 acres sold for $1,540.

At the end of 1839, Daniel bought two parcels of land in his own name. He undoubtedly sought an investment that would generate another source of income, but he also may have wanted land that was not part of the former James estate. Daniel used money from the James trust fund to purchase from Benjamin Wofford's sister, Rebecca Wofford Mullinax, a pricey eight acres on the Tyger River that included a "mill and shoal." This probably was a water-powered grist mill, likely run by slave labor that may have included Mason's youngest child, Sam.

Daniel was taken to court three times in 1841, and the judgments against him totaled more than $3,000. There must have been times when Jane wondered whether they were going to be able to keep their property. Mason and Rachael undoubtedly felt the uncertainty as well, for they and their children were pawns in the bitter feud.

After 1841, though, there appears to have been no further civil cases filed against Daniel. He was granted citizenship, for which he originally had petitioned on October 9, 1832.

Whether Daniel was a man of questionable character with an altered past or just an innocent victim of circumstance is unclear. It does appear that his marriage to Jane, over the objections of the Austins, began a chain reaction of legal trouble. As for Trotting Sally's grandmother, Mason, the Mullins marriage made a lasting impact on her family for generations to come.

14

4

Mason's youngest child, Samuel, was born in 1827. Just who his father was cannot be determined. Mason's last known childbirth prior to that took place about six years earlier, before John James died. This implies that Samuel may have had a different father than the rest of Mason's children. It is also possible that one of the male slaves that Austin seized when he forced Jane to give up part of her estate in 1829 could have been the father.

Being the youngest of six children, Samuel may have been favored. On many farms, even very young slave children played a role in the labor force. That role expanded as they got older. Samuel was young, strong and quick-witted — willing to do any chore. He may have worked as a servant to Daniel, helping at the gristmill and cotton gin and accompanying him on trips to town to pick up supplies. He took the opportunity to engage himself in learning everything he could about farming, which would serve him the rest of his life.

Even slaves were aware that scratching out a living was a struggle for many upcountry cotton farmers. Poor farming practices and the vagaries of weather, along with the addition of new Southern states and territories that glutted the cotton market, kept profits at a minimum. In the 1820s and 1830s, tariffs placed on imported goods nearly ignited a civil war and made living expenses even higher. Proud farmers were plagued by a cycle of debt. With consecutive bad years, farmers ran the risk of losing everything.

Daniel and Jane continued to struggle financially until Daniel died in 1844. The cause of his death is unknown. Records indicate that he owed $3,000 when he died without a will. At least part of this $3,000 may have been from the 1841 court judgments against him.

For several years after Daniel's death, Jane continued to manage the farm. She had her hands full handling several hundred acres of land, more than 50 head of hogs, six horses, two wagons, a cotton gin and the old Mullinax mill.

Daniel's legal and financial woes did not end with his death. Even though he had not legally owned the farm, as administrator he owed money that would have jeopardized Jane's holdings to the land and other property. The court-appointed administrator of Daniel's estate, John Bomar Jr., took Jane to court over rents and profits from the two parcels of land that Daniel purchased by himself and, in the years following Daniel's death, Jane was named as defendant in several equity cases. Austin also continued to pursue legal action. For Jane, at 61 years old, marrying again was out of the question.

In 1848, she offered the property to Austin. She likely saw it as the only way to retain her home. Her son in law and daughter seized the moment by offering Jane a deal she could not afford to pass up. They would pay all her debt and allow her to spend her remaining years on the plantation, provided she deeded the farm — land, house, equipment, livestock, buildings and slaves — to Thomas.

The deed states, "In consideration of love and affection which I bear to my son in law... also for $1 paid by [him] ... I have sold all my tracts of land on which I now live... for payment of all my debts ... and then for decent and comfortable support of myself during my life."

Mason and her family were now Austin's legal property.

Despite those sentiments, Jane probably remained distant and never reconciled with her daughter. Jane James Mullins was strong willed – she had to be. Three years after she gave up her land, the S.C. Court of Appeals issued the final ruling in the tug of war over the profits from the Mullinax and Foster tracts of land that Daniel had bought in late 1839 and early 1840. The former James slaves, Mason and Rachael, played a central role in the precedent-setting dispute, which was cited in a South Carolina case as recently as 2013 and by Harvard Law Review.

The appellate court noted the legal history of the Mullins' estate: how Daniel had granted administrative rights to a trustee to all property and any profits from it that he had gained by marrying Jane several months earlier. The 1829 agreement contained a crucial element — that Jane would be allowed to dispose of two-thirds of the property and convey once more the other third back to Daniel.

After Daniel's death, Jane retained the former Mullinax and Foster properties on the basis that Daniel had bought them with money from her trust fund. Bomar sued Jane over profits from these properties — in particular, most likely, the gristmill.

Though Daniel himself was gone, his character was addressed squarely in the case, and he was presented as "drunken, indolent and unthrifty." The original court had supported Jane's argument that her money had paid for the Mullinax and Foster tracts. "From the evidence as to the means and habits of Daniel Mullins ... I conclude that the payments were made from the trust funds. It did appear that most of the labor and expense in erecting and repairing the mill and dam on the Mullinax tract was furnished and expended from the trust estate. Daniel Mullins exercised some supervision in the erection and repair of the mills [sic], and in the management of the plantation, but in the latter particular, at least, the defendant was the more efficient manager... Mullins, at his death in 1844, left unpaid large liabilities ... [bearing] no connection to the trust estate... D. Mullins is utterly insolvent, unless these two tracts of land are made liable for his debts."

Bomar sued, claiming that there was no proof that the trust funds were used for the purchases and that Daniel's one-third profits as laid out in the 1829 deal could have provided him with money for the purchases.

The appellate court noted that John James had willed to Jane "two negroes absolutely," Rachael and Mason, and in considering the thorny question of what Daniel had in "vested interest or remainder" at his death set the two women aside as "absolutely belonging to Jane Mullins."

In summing up its ruling, the appeals court said, "We concur ... that D. Mullins is not entitled to a present interest of one-third of the estate conveyed by his deed. It would be a preposterous construction, which would give him a right to immediate re-conveyance of one-third of the estate, when he expressly gives the whole to his wife for life, and also gives to her the right to dispose of two-thirds thereof by will. His claim to the re-conveyance of one-third is subject and subsequent to these rights of the wife.

"It is ordered and decreed, that the decree be affirmed, and the appeal be dismissed."

Through all of this, it appears that Mason and perhaps some of her children remained with Jane. The slave schedule censuses indicate that Austin sent Samuel and other slaves to work his plantation in Greenville and did not farm the Mullins plantation. This probably separated Mason from her children. Austin may have leased it or bargained with other local farmers for use of the land.

.

5

The life of a slave in the upcountry varied. Labor, living, social and environmental conditions depended on the humanity, wealth and generosity of the owner. Some slaves worked as domestic servants and lived in the main house. Otherwise, they lived with or in similar circumstances to the field hands in cabins or shacks in the slave quarters. These dwellings, often crudely constructed, were cold in the winter and hot in the summer.

In the 1850 slave schedule, Austin is recorded as the owner of 51 slaves. He housed most of them in nine dwellings at Oakland. In the same census year, Jane reported having 17 slaves, which suggests that Austin may have given or allowed her the use of slaves after he obtained her property and paid her debts. Most of Austin's slaves were young adults suited for fieldwork. Jane's slaves consisted of three middle-aged males for heavy work around the farm; older and middle-aged women, likely including Mason and Rachael; a few young females of child-bearing age and seven young children.

Mason's youngest child, Samuel, now worked at Oakland plantation. He would have been approximately 21 years old — too valuable a field hand to stay with Jane. He spent long hours laboring in the hot sun, chopping and picking cotton and doing many other backbreaking chores. Separated from his mother, he may have been afforded the opportunity to visit her at the Mullins farm from time to time. In fact, Austin likely visited Jane on a regular basis. Sam may have traveled with him.

During this time, Sam began "sparking" with a young woman named Rachael, who is not to be confused with Mason's longtime co-worker. It appears they met after 1848, so Rachael may have been one of Austin's slaves.

By law, it was illegal for slaves to marry, yet some did have ceremonies. In order for slaves to unite, they needed approval from their masters. With that approval, Sam and Rachael "jumped the broom" sometime around 1849. Marriage was a legal contract that slaves were not permitted to have, so this informal vow did not prevent one or the other from being sold at the whim of their masters.

Rachael began having children in 1850. She had 11 live births, according to the 1900 census, but all did not survive. Her first two children were girls — Harriet, born in 1850, and Laura, born in 1852. Then in 1856, possibly in the summer, Sam and Rachael had their first son. They named him George. Three more children would follow: Billy in 1858, Sam Jr. in 1859 and Mason in 1860. Twelve years later another daughter, Rachael, was born free.

6

During the 1850s many Southerners strongly favored the idea of disunion, especially South Carolinians. John C. Calhoun, a prominent South Carolina politician, became known as the father of the secession movement. As new territories sprang up in the West, the issues of slavery and states' rights helped fuel the talk of war. Many slave-holding Southerners were convinced that Northern politicians under pressure from abolitionists would do away with the slave system, which the South saw as essential to its agricultural and economic survival.

On November 6, 1860, Abraham Lincoln was elected president. South Carolina unanimously voted to secede from the Union on December 20, and other states soon followed. Though Citadel cadets fired the first shots of the conflict in January 1861, it was the bombardment of Fort Sumter in April that triggered all-out war.

The conflict quickly brought many changes to the upcountry for both master and slave. The Piedmont region endured disruptions, shortages and changes in social structure and leadership. Many young men from the upcountry enlisted in the state militia to defend their home state against an invading enemy. With the exception of a base at Port Royal and raids along the coast to disrupt the movement of supplies, South Carolina remained free of Union invasion until 1865.

It is not clear whether Sam and Rachael lived together when the war began. If she had children during the war, they did not survive. She and Sam also may have been separated during this time. The conflict attributed to many changes in their lives. It likely siphoned some slave labor from the plantation, which meant that Sam may have worked longer hours. The female slaves may have helped with the war industry on the textile front as well. Many essentials were in short supply.

Sam's visits, if any, to the Mullins farm were few and far between. Slaves like Sam and Rachael simply focused on survival from day to day, while praying for an end to the bloody war. The concept of freedom was so alien that some slaves could not comprehend it. While some saw it as a blessing, others feared its yawning uncertainty.

In 1862, an important event set in motion a number of swift changes. In March, at the age of 73, Jane James Mullins died. For several years she had been in the close care of her second cousin, Maiden Smith. Jane stayed under her own roof, though, apparently determined never to live under Austin's.

Jane had no legal property, so a will was not recorded. Any personal property went to Polly.

During the early 1830s Jane had joined Brushy Creek Baptist Church, located in Greenville District. There is no indication that Daniel was a member. As a domestic slave, Mason may have attended church with Jane. In 1848, Jane had transferred her membership to Mount Zion Baptist Church in Spartanburg District, less than a mile from her home.

She was buried at Mount Zion, where her headstone was dedicated by her daughter. It read, "Jane James wife of John James." The Mullins name was left out.

Local historian Dr. J.B.O. Landrum also omitted the Mullins name when writing about Jane in his "History of Spartanburg County," first published in 1900. Landrum revealed that he grew up near "Mrs. James" and became "acquainted with her excellent traits of character... Owning at the time a valuable negro property, she possessed an indomitable will, was excellent in management, possessing, as she did, splendid judgment. Being of a superior mind, she was fond of reading, and had a remarkable memory. She was kind and hospitable in her home, and enjoyed having young people visit her. She was good to the poor and devoted to the church and loved to have ministers of the Gospel visit."

Jane's passing was likely bittersweet for Samuel. He would have been saddened by her death. After all, he had known her his entire life. Perhaps she had been good to him and treated his mother with grace and dignity. Now Miss Jane was gone.

Her death may have produced one positive change for his family. If Samuel's mother still was living, as she appeared to be in the 1860 slave schedule, she would have been moved to Oakland. With Mason on the Oakland plantation, Samuel now would have his family in one place. Likely he wondered from time to time what would become of the Mullins farm and whether he ever would see it again.

By the summer of 1863, the Confederacy had suffered a number of ill-fated setbacks that would determine the outcome of the war. In an effort to bring the war to a stalemate,

General Robert E. Lee invaded the North with his mighty Army of Northern Virginia. He was met head on by a decisive Union victory at Gettysburg. The loss of Vicksburg was another bitter blow against the South, as was the evacuation of Chattanooga. In August, Fort Sumter was relentlessly reduced to rubble by a bombardment from Union batteries on nearby Morris Island. Soon Charleston was under constant fire from a newly installed 8-inch Parrott rifle nicknamed the "Swamp Angel." News of other losses ran rampant throughout the South. Union victories such as these sealed the Confederacy's fate.

The war brought changes to rich and poor alike. Thomas and Polly Austin had 11 children. Of their five sons, three served in the Confederate Army, with one paying the ultimate price. Laurence Manning Austin attended Wofford College for a year before getting his medical degree from Tulane University. He served as a field surgeon in the 13th Mississippi Infantry Regiment and died back home of disease on July 19, 1863.

Josiah Thomas Austin also attended Wofford before enlisting in Manigault's Battalion. After the war, he served in the S.C. House of Representatives and S.C. Senate. He also led the Greenville County Democratic Party.

Family history says that William Austin also served, attaining the rank of lieutenant. In all, eight Austin men from Oakland and Gilder plantations provided military service to the Confederacy.

Before the war, Thomas Austin was a successful planter with many holdings. He had a large cotton plantation, with slaves to work the land. He was a pillar of the community and a respected leader. With the Confederacy's hopes dwindling he, like many of his contemporaries, looked for ways to protect and conceal his wealth. In 1860, his personal estate had been valued in the census at $49,500. Slaves made up a portion of this, which he stood to lose if the Confederacy fell. In early October 1863, Austin sold the Mullins property to cotton agent James S. Gibbs of Charleston for $8,000 and nearly wiped Daniel's footprint from Spartanburg County. Did Mason and her children shake their heads and mutter among themselves at the news? Jane had gone on, but it had been their home as well, and now it was gone, too.

Stress on the home front increased in 1864, as it did on soldiers in the field. Rumors flew in the upcountry of bands of roving deserters. News reports provided no comfort, and masters and slaves alike began to sense that the end was near. Local women, left as heads of household with their husbands off at war, began to fear their slaves, who grew bolder as the Confederacy weakened.

In 1865, the war truly came to South Carolina's doorstep. On February 17, General William Tecumseh Sherman's army stormed into Columbia, leaving the capital in ashes. African-American regiments, some of which contained former Lowcountry slaves, were among the Union units that next occupied Charleston. On April 2, Confederate President Jefferson Davis, along with senior members of his government — and the last of the Confederate Treasury's gold and silver — fled Richmond. He went south and entered the Palmetto State in York County on April 26, then traveled through Union on his way toward Abbeville and Georgia.

Sherman's army pressed swiftly on to Lancaster, Camden and Cheraw and eventually into North Carolina. The same day that Davis entered South Carolina, Confederate General Joseph E. Johnston surrendered in North Carolina.

On April 29, Union troops chasing Davis entered Spartanburg and stayed for three days. Soldiers captured Davis on May 10 near Irwinville, Georgia. Though the last Confederate commanders did not surrender until months later, the war effectively was over.

7

News of the Confederacy's collapse came in a rash of dreadful reports. For the upcountry, there were no invading armies destroying crops and decimating infrastructure as in other parts of the state. Like a terrible blizzard, Sherman's destructive path from Columbia to Goldsboro had come and gone. What was left in his path was a wasteland. Columbia had been completely destroyed, leaving the state without a central government. Charleston was a ghost town with heavy damage to buildings, warehouses and homes. Roads, bridges, railroads, farms and cotton gins had been destroyed. Lawlessness was everywhere. Many farms were abandoned, and roads were flooded with refugees. Food and other goods were scarce. Poor whites were near starvation. Slaves in the path of Sherman's forces had been told they were free but had nowhere to go and no means of getting there. Federal troops came and went in the upcountry, often adding to the anarchy by strong-arm thievery.

In the upcountry, the war's end did not bring immediate freedom to African Americans. Crops needed care, same as always, no matter the labor situation. In early June, a federal proclamation was issued that freed all slaves, but some up-country slave owners chose to ignore it. In August, a second order specified that masters must tell their slaves that they were free, and that they must be paid if they perform work.

Austin was one of those who procrastinated. Just how long he waited is unknown, but as time passed he was pressured to tell his slaves the truth.

Among those who tended to the needs of the Austin plantation were two white sisters, Margaret and Amanda Vaughn. They worked as weavers and seamstresses and made most of the clothes for the Austin family. Margaret became agitated after the war that Austin had not emancipated his slaves. One day she simply took matters into her own hands. The petite woman took Austin out to the cotton fields and waved a white piece of cloth to signal the workers to gather. One at a time they came and stood. As Austin silently looked on, Margaret told the slaves that they were free. The field hands gaped at Austin until one brave soul asked, "You mean we can go?" Aunt Mag, as she was known, sharply replied that Austin had no say in the matter — they were free.

Ironically, Margaret Vaughn's nephew, Martin Vaughn, purchased Oakland in 1897. She and her sister lived there the rest of their days.

Some of Austin's newly freed slaves undoubtedly left, though he probably offered them a place to stay if they continued to work on the plantation. The U.S. Freedmen's Bureau began overseeing labor contracts between former masters and slaves in the region as early as autumn 1865. Postwar census documentation shows that many Austin freedmen lived near his plantation and worked as sharecroppers.

Sam faced an agonizing decision. He had longed to return to Beech Springs, but the Mullins place was gone. He likely stayed on at the Austin farm through the fall and winter, working under contract. Possibly as early as the spring of 1866, he gathered his loved ones and returned to the vicinity of his childhood home. As a free man he felt proud and triumphant to see Beech Springs again.

Just imagine the line of freed people — men with their head held high as women tended to the straggling children — as they filed off the Austin plantation and headed northeast toward the county line.

The issue of Reconstruction in South Carolina is much too complex to discuss briefly. A new social class and political system grew out of the postwar period. For the newly emancipated, Reconstruction was a series of steps forward in the political, social, economic, educational and religious arenas. For the first time African Americans could vote, run for and hold offices, own property, sit on juries and testify to them, and participate in law enforcement as constables and militia. Yet most freedoms gained slowly eroded when Southern Democrats and moderates regained power in the late 1870s. For most African Americans, the road to freedom had just begun.

In the first years after the war, most freedmen did not venture far in their work as contracted paid laborers. As such, they were at the mercy of the landowners. The majority of freedmen didn't own land, crops, tools or working animals. Sam would have worked long hours for little pay.

As a sharecropper, with help from the Freedmen's Bureau, Sam would have contracted for one-year seasons. His tools, seed and supplies were likely supplied by the one he contracted with — the landowner. At the end of the growing season, crops would have been divided, as outlined by the contract.

This process would have been repeated for the following season. Sam would have bartered with local farmers for other needs and wants.

In 1867, it was required by law that all freedmen take a surname. A popular misconception exists that most freedmen took the last name of their former masters. However, this was not always the case. As free people, many former slaves chose other names. It was not uncommon for freedmen to adopt one surname, only to change it later. Many of Austin's former slaves who located near him did in fact take the Austin name.

Sam, on the other hand, settled in Beech Springs and chose Mullins.

What was behind his choice? After all, Daniel Mullins had died some 23 years earlier and left no significant legacy. His name had been left off Jane's grave marker. Daniel's only property had been obtained through marrying Jane. He had no formal title and held no political office. He had never been called on to witness deeds, and there are no records that imply he ever had been a member of any church, society or political group. However, Sam had toiled and sweated on this piece of land commonly referred to as the Mullins plantation – the likely place of his birth. It was in his blood.

In addition, the Mullins and Austin slaves may have quietly chosen sides during Austin's sustained antagonism toward Mullins. Sam's mother had been Jane's personal servant. She would have been privy to private conversations and known far more about the affair than field hands. She also would have known how the terrible infighting affected Jane.

Daniel, for all his possible faults, was from a different place with a more progressive attitude toward slavery. His attitude toward slaves may have differed markedly from Austin's. Sam probably knew some of the lengths that Austin went to in order to disengage Mullins from both Jane and her estate: how he had Daniel jailed for polygamy and how he had repeatedly made claims to his mother in-law's property; how he had ended up with everything, which left her at his mercy. Sam saw firsthand how Daniel and Jane had struggled over the years to make ends meet.

Then, in 1848, Sam became Austin's field slave. He likely worked long backbreaking hours in the field. He may have seen Jane's headstone. He wouldn't have been able to read it but was likely told that the Mullins name was not on it. Also, as mentioned earlier, there is another possibility to consider. One of the male slaves taken by Austin in 1829 may have been Samuel's father. If so, Samuel may have blamed Austin for splitting up his parents.

There is one more possibility to consider: Could Mullins have fathered Samuel? The only problem is the timeline. It appears that Daniel had not been in the area long when he married Jane, and at that time Samuel would have been about 15 months old.

On the other hand, Sam's mother had spent most of her days on the James/Mullins plantation. Perhaps just as Jane had felt ownership, even after she granted the farm to her son-in-law, Sam also may have felt a heritage from the land and name. Samuel likely chose Mullins because he felt connected, and it gave him a real sense of identity. He was a Mullins by birthright — connected to the land he loved.

The family appears to have jointly decided that their surname would reflect their time with Daniel and Jane. Also taking the Mullins surname were Sam's possible uncle, Patrick; Sam's brother, Robert; and their nephew, Ellin's son Jackson. Samuel, Jackson and Patrick each gave this surname when they registered as voters in 1868.

No matter the cause, Sam could have stayed in Greenville but he didn't. He left and carried on the Mullins name.

The 1870 census places Samuel and family living near John Shores' farm and Jacob Frey's residence and tannery in the vicinity of what is now U.S. Highway 29, west of Spartanburg. Frey's property was adjacent to the old Mullins farm, which by then was owned by Gibbs. Samuel, who had lived in the area at least since 1868, may have sharecropped for one of these white property owners.

In the census, Mullins reported having tangible assets of $100, and a live-in laborer named Perry Stephens. It appears that compared with other freedmen, Samuel was a successful farmer with a sizable amount of personal assets. In other words, Sam was doing quite well.

Perhaps Samuel had plans to purchase farm property — maybe to own a few acres of the old plantation lands where he grew up. He never got that chance, due in part to the fact that many white landowners were opposed to freedmen owning property. After Reconstruction, Sam's modest assets simply dwindled.

As for Mason, her fate is unknown. Evidence suggests she died before 1870. Jane claimed a 66-year-old female on the 1860 slave schedule, and this matches Mason's age as it was given in the Hawkins paperwork. The 1870 census does not list Mason. If living, it would seem she would have lived with one of her children. Mason was born in the mid-1790s. She had served as a domestic slave, raised children and grandchildren and had seen a lifetime of changes, hard times and struggles. Perhaps she did live to see the chains of slavery lifted and spent her last days as a free person — owned by no one.

If Mason died before Jane's death in 1862, she would have been buried at the Mullins place. If she passed sometime after, yet before the end of the war, she likely was buried in Greenville. Mason may have been buried at the slave cemetery once located at Austin's father's residence near Gilder. On the other hand, as a freedwoman, Mason could have been laid to rest almost anywhere. Perhaps she rests in the cemetery of the old Foster's Meeting House adjacent to the Mullins plantation.

8

George was about 9 years old in the summer of 1865. Freedom hadn't made life any easier. The exhausting work of sharecropping didn't seem that different from the labor at Oakland plantation. In some ways, things seemed the same. With the occasional exception on Sundays, there were no days off. His mother may have required that he go to church, which was a break from the everyday cycle of chores. He plowed and planted in the spring and chopped cotton during the long, hot summers. As fall approached, he picked cotton from first light to sundown. Considering his height and age, George would have been an excellent picker. Children didn't have to bend over, their hands were small and they possessed endless energy. At day's end, George likely picked well over 150 pounds of cotton. Late fall into winter he helped chop wood, cleaned and repaired tools and mended fences. Given the opportunity, he may have labored on neighboring farms as well. He was never without work.

George was an important factor in helping his family in the postwar years. During this time, George's unique energy and friendly personality began to blossom. Keeping busy would have suited him. He likely met no strangers and constantly talked to himself, all the while skipping, singing and trotting to his next chore. He seemed to never tire. This personality trait favored him, and others noticed it.

According to legend, it was around this time that George acquired the nickname that would follow him the rest of his life. It is said that as a child he saw a horse named Sally trotting down the road. Young George went trotting after or alongside the horse. Some stories have him actually outrunning the horse. From that day on, George was referred to as "Trotting Sally." There are variations on this story, yet all feature him racing a horse named Sally. In later years, Trotting Sally would claim that he was part horse — gesturing and pawing the ground and even neighing.

On the other hand, the definition of the verb "sally" should be considered. It means to leap forward, which may suggest an altogether different manner in which he came about his name. It could be that local white people who didn't know his real name simply referred to him as the strange-acting fellow who trotted and sallied.

Another rare folktale provides a different motivation for his endless energy and unusual behavior. Just prior to his birth, his mother, Rachael, was riding in a horse-drawn wagon or carriage when a dog began barking and snipping at the horse, frightening the animal. It started kicking, bucking and running out of control, which startled his mother. Some say that this single event "marked" George, creating his colorful personality and energetic spirit that motivated him to paw and neigh like a horse, as well as bark like a dog.

George continued to live and work with his family during most of the 1870s. Sometime prior to 1880, he and his cousin, Robert Mullins, left home to share a place in Spartanburg

Township and work as farm laborers. This younger Robert was Ellin's grandson by her son, Jackson. The two young men lived adjacent to James Wood, a white farmer, and may have worked for him. This put them north of the city limits by the Pacolet River.

The urge to get out on his own, to see something new, had started to take hold of George.

Around this same time, George took a shine to a young African-American woman by the name of Lizzie Gilliam. Just how they met is unknown. The two apparently were married shortly after the 1880 census. Records suggest Lizzie may have been as young as 10 years old when she gave birth to their first child, a son they named Charlie, sometime between 1880 and 1882. She almost certainly was older, though – perhaps around 15 — as her age varied wildly from census to census.

A rare tale says that George rushed to get a doctor after Lizzie went into labor. He soon arrived at the doctor's house. The physician quickly grabbed his medical bag and offered the expectant father a ride back in his buggy. Trotting Sally refused the ride, preferring to trot home the same way he came. When the doctor arrived, Trotting Sally was already there waiting on the porch.

A story collected from oral family lore has it that George would pull his wife and children in a wagon or buggy in place of a horse or mule to church service on Sunday mornings, sometimes neighing along the way.

On January 20, 1883, one of the bastions of George's childhood died. Dr. Thomas Collins Austin had loomed large in the lives of the former James and Mullins slaves. The Methodist publication the Southern Christian Advocate paid homage to

Austin several weeks after his death at the age of 93, calling him a "great and good man" and a "born leader."

"He was of the highest type of ante-bellum South Carolina gentleman," the memorial notice continued. "...He was devoted to the Church of his choice, a truly pious, humble holy man for several years previous to his death. On account of his great age, he was confined to his house, and later to his room... He met death resignedly, and his end was peaceful."

Whether George knew of the death is unknown, but Austin was one of the last people left who had held the fate of Trotting Sally's family in his hand.

George and Lizzie had their own lives now and, as much as poverty and prejudice would allow, were masters of their own fates. They had at least five other children. Like many people of this period, they and their children were illiterate. They had no means to record birthdates and, possibly, saw no reason to do so. As a result, their children's ages tended to vary census to census by a few years. Richard was born about 1883. Their first and only daughter, Riller, was born about 1891. Barney was born about 1894 and Edward about '97. Their last child, Matthew, was born about 1902.

The family's whereabouts are sketchy from the early 1880s to the turn of the century, in part due to a fire that destroyed most of the 1890 federal census records. The 1900 census reports George and his growing family lived in Beech Springs. He was a farm laborer.

This does not discount the possibility that he picked up other work from time to time. He may have found work in nearby Lyman, Wellford or Spartanburg. With new building construction going on in the area, it is likely that he began working as a laborer at some of these sites. His first experience at construction may have been at the Tucapau cotton mill (sometimes called "Turkey-Paw"), which was located near the town of Wellford on the Middle Tyger River. It was completed in 1896. There is no documentation to support this theory, but he lived close by, needed the work and would have taken most any job.

Grays Creek runs through the old John James land, now covered in scrub brush, saplings and mature trees.

John Fowler

After John James died, his widow Jane inherited the property in western Spartanburg County, now bisected by Interstate 85 and bordered by Mount Zion, Falling Creek and Fort Prince roads. She later married a newcomer to the area named Daniel Mullins. This land also was home to an extended African-American slave family that took the surname Mullins after the end of the Civil War.

Photo courtesy of YMCA of Greenville, Hollingsworth Outdoor Center

Sharecroppers work a field at Oakland Plantation, circa 1898. Dr. Thomas Collins Austin built the house in the background in 1823 after marrying the daughter of John and Jane James, Mary "Polly" Turner James. George Mullins was born a slave on this property near Simpsonville, South Carolina, in 1856.

LeighAnn Snuggs

The house at the old Oakland Plantation as it looked in May 2013. The YMCA of Greenville uses the property as a living-history site, the Hollingsworth Outdoor Center.

Author John Thomas Fowler, right, researches Oakland's history at the Hollingsworth Outdoor Center.

LeighAnn Snuggs

The site of Austin's medical office on Oakland has been excavated. In addition to his paying customers, Austin probably treated slaves here. This also may have been where at least some slaves gave birth.

LeighAnn Snuggs

Numerous outbuildings remain at the Hollingsworth center from the old Oakland Plantation.

LeighAnn Snuggs

Slaves cut and notched logs to build this Oakland barn and also made the trough that still hangs in it.

After Jane died in 1862, her daughter dedicated a gravestone at Mount Zion Baptist Church Cemetery that made no mention of Jane's second marriage to Daniel Mullins.

John Fowler

Jane's gravestone has since been broken in two. The verse on
it is from Job 19:25-26: "For I know that my redeemer liveth,
and that he shall stand at the latter day upon the earth: And
though after my skin worms destroy this body, yet in my
flesh shall I see God." (AV)

52

J.D. Collins Department Store's utilization of Trotting Sally in this advertisement illustrates how well known a character Mullins was in the area. This pre-Thanksgiving ad ran in the Spartanburg Herald on November 11, 1923. This was the same year that Spartanburg photographer Alfred T. Willis took the famous photo of George that appears on the cover. The ad is enlarged here for legibility.

THINKS HE'S A HORSE.

"Trotting Sally," Col. McKinley Says, Is the Spriest Negro Extant.

Col. Gordon McKinley of South Carolina and Col. Henry Ormsby of North Carolina were seated in the Hoffman House yesterday afternoon discussing the race question from the point of view of the "two Carolina Governors." They had a large and attentive audience, and the stories they told ranged all the way from the mythical Negro Judge who charged the jury "25 cents a head" to the Republican darkies of Charleston who, in 1876 gave up their registration tickets for passes to a circus, claiming that the citizen's duty of voting should be secondary to his pleasure at seeing "the elephant and the clown."

Finally the talk became somewhat serious, and McKinley, who was recently in the very prosperous City of Spartanburg, S. C., told the story of "Trotting Sally," the negro who is famous from Fort Moultrie to the Blue Ridge Mountains as the happiest and hardest working negro in the Palmetto State.

"Very few persons in Spartanburg," said Col. McKinley, "know that 'Trotting Sally's' right name is Roach. The only name they know him by is his race-horse appellation. 'Trotting Sally' is a day laborer and he is never without work. He always works in a trot and never seems to tire.

"'Trotting Sally' thinks that he is a horse, and when he is at work he throws back his head, inflates his chest, and gives a snort like a four-year-old in a seven-furlong dash.

"The violin also plays an important part in the everyday life of Sally, and he's never seen without his fiddle and bow strapped across his back. At the dinner hour he eats, jumps, and plays by turns. He is never still a moment, and according to some of the other negroes who know him, he even dances in his sleep. Yes, indeed, he's a wonderful negro.

"How did he get his name? Oh, that's easy. One day, they say, when Sally was a very small boy, a farmer who owned a fast horse was on his way to town. Sally saw the buggy dash past his mammy's hut, and from that moment he has imagined that he is a horse. After the buggy ran Sally. At the end of a mile he had overtaken the wagon. It was ten miles to Spartanburg, but Sally outran the horse, and was a mile in the lead when he passed the town limits."

"I have nothing to say for publication," murmured Col. Ormsby when Col. McKinley had finished.

The New York Times featured Trotting Sally in its February 25, 1907, edition – a rare accomplishment for an African American from the small-town South during the Jim Crow era. Though racially insensitive and incorrect in parts, it offers a fascinating glimpse of Mullins and his renown "from Fort Moultrie to the Blue Ridge Mountains" and beyond.

Courtesy of the Herald-Journal Willis Collection,
Spartanburg County Public Libraries

Alfred T. Willis filmed George performing on the street. This frame captured from the moving picture shows him playing his fiddle, Rosalie.

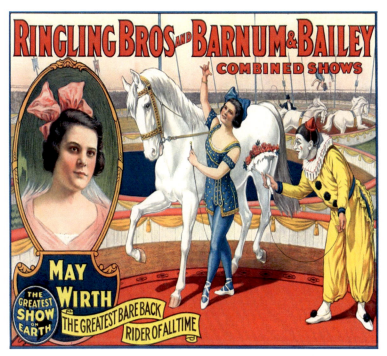

The time frame of the Willis film clip can be narrowed down
substantially by the Ringling Bros. and Barnum & Bailey
billboard that George partially obscures. The Strobridge
Lithographing Company created this billboard or poster in 1924,
and Ringling and Barnum & Bailey appears to have used it
through May Wirth's final season with the circus in 1927. Willis
probably filmed George in 1927, when he was busy filming
events such as celebrated pilot Charles Lindbergh's visit to
Spartanburg.

Courtesy of the Herald-Journal Willis Collection, Spartanburg County Public Libraries

In another frame captured from the Willis film clip, George draws a small crowd.

Courtesy of the Herald-Journal Willis Collection,
Spartanburg County Public Libraries

George ends his performance with a signature move, howling or barking at onlookers, at the end of the act that Willis caught on film.

The Paper

George lived in this cabin in the Mud Creek area of Boiling Springs in his later years. He died alone here on September 20, 1931.

LeighAnn Snuggs

The cemetery at Ridgeville Baptist Church, where George is buried among family.

LeighAnn Snuggs

John Henry Mullins is another member of the Mullins family buried at Ridgeville. He was the oldest child of George's oldest child, Charlie.

George's great-grandson, Alfred Mullins, owns Mullins Cleaners in Landrum.

LeighAnn Snuggs

Alfred proudly displays a copy of the Willis photograph in his business. He is the fourth generation of first sons in the Mullins line that traces directly back to his paternal great-grandfather, George.

9

In the late night hours of June 5, 1903, torrential rains began to fall across the Piedmont. Heavy downpours continued throughout the night. Streams and rivers overflowed along low-lying areas, making some roads and bridges impassable. Soon homes and farms were threatened. As morning approached, events worsened. The Pacolet River swelled to a monstrous size of death and destruction, taking with it everything in its path.

As the sun rose early the next day and the deluge subsided, locals were horrified at the loss of life and property. The five-story Clifton Mill No. 3, also known as Converse, and its dam gave way to the rampaging water. Three quarters of a mile downstream Clifton Mill No. 1 took the brunt of the force, which destroyed most of the mill and a great deal of the mill village. The fury also took nearly half of Clifton Mill No. 2 and with it Santuck, a small bundle of homes in a low-lying area where most of the lives were lost. As daylight approached downstream, many locals were able to escape to higher ground. Helplessly they watched as Pacolet Mill No.1, a four-story 30,000-spindle mill, went crashing into the swollen river. Within an hour, Pacolet No. 2 succumbed to the raging water, and No. 3 also was severely damaged. By the time the worst was over, at least 67 lives had been lost, leaving hundreds homeless.

Other parts of Spartanburg County also received heavy damage due to the storm. Bridges and roads were washed away. Neighbors lost livestock, barns, automobiles, storage buildings, cotton gins, crops, grain mills and houses. Mary Louise, a small cotton mill located near Cowpens, was completely destroyed. Part of the Fingerville Cotton Mill was badly damaged, and the iron bridge at Fingerville swept away. Countless miles of rails throughout the county were washed out or damaged. The main Southern Railway trestle over Lawson's Fork Creek broke free. Every bridge on the road between Spartanburg and Boiling Springs was wrecked or simply gone. Hall's Bridge in New Prospect and the bridge at Clark's Mill near Inman were lost, and the dam at Inman Mills was carried away. Many farmers reported their crops completely destroyed, which devastated the local agricultural economy.

Rescue operations soon gave way to cleanup and recovery efforts. From the early stages, many African Americans were employed in the harsh task of cleanup. The work — a great deal done by hand — was dangerous, demanding and very hard. For weeks, crews uncovered machine parts, wood and debris, trees, bricks and other materials, along with personal belongings and an occasional badly decomposed body that usually was beyond the point of identification. Anything of worth was salvaged, cotton being the most important. Bales that had been washed downstream were retrieved. Flooded warehouses were emptied. On July 17, more than 1,000 bales of cotton were unearthed in the sand along the banks of the Pacolet River. The find was valued at more than $60,000.

There is no evidence to support that George participated in the initial cleanup efforts, yet local history does place him in Pacolet Mills working as a construction laborer. He worked with bricklayers on the construction site of Pacolet Mill No. 5. This mill replaced the other two that were lost in the flood. He boarded with a Native American named Will "French" Finch at Point Lookout, located near No. 5. In the 1910 federal census, Finch still lived in Pacolet. He worked as a textile operative and lived with his wife and children.

A popular tale of Trotting Sally falling from a scaffold likely originated in Pacolet. His job was to keep brickmasons supplied with bricks. Some say he was always full of energy, even neighing like a horse as he pushed his heavy wheelbarrow along the unstable narrow boards. The story has it that one day he lost his footing and fell to the ground. Just how high he was no one remembers, yet the legend says he was not hurt and continued with his work with the same energy and enthusiasm.

Exactly how long Trotting Sally spent in Pacolet is a mystery. He may have worked a short while and returned to his family in Beech Springs, yet oral history suggests that he stayed in the area much longer. In fact, stories have him working in the area as a farm laborer several years after the flood. Area folklore places him, at least part of the time, living in a little shack or shanty on Jerusalem Road in an African-American community near Pacolet.

Another reason he may have stayed was that he saw no reason to return. It appears that his mother and father passed away sometime between 1900 and 1910. George may have felt beholden to his parents. Samuel and Rachael were in their late 70s by 1900. Sam was a proud man. He had seen so much change in his lifetime. He was born a slave, toiled in the hot sun, worked as a sharecropper and tenant farmer, and raised children, grandchildren and great-grandchildren. He and Rachael had been married for decades. They must have played a big role in keeping their son grounded, at least most of the time. Once they passed, Trotting Sally felt free, as if he had no standards left to meet. He may have simply left and never returned to Beech Springs, abandoning Lizzie and the children.

10

By the turn of the century, Trotting Sally was already a well-known character. He was noticed wherever he went. Spartans swapped stories about the man who would paw the ground and neigh, saying, "He thinks he's a horse!" When he worked, he labored at a speedy pace, hardly ever slowing. Some would say, "He even dances in his sleep" and add, "Pay him twice what you are paying the others, 'cause he's doing twice the work."

George moved to the city of Spartanburg sometime prior to 1910. After working construction in Pacolet he simply followed the work, possibly as early as 1905. At the time, Spartanburg was experiencing a boom in building. On occasion disaster struck, like the "Big Fire" in 1907 on Forest Street that destroyed more than 70 residences and buildings. Day laborers, many of them African American, would have been employed for the dirty, dangerous cleanup work.

The 1910 federal census documents George as a boarder of Carrie Gillam [sic], who resided at 119 Thompson Street within the city limits. Carrie was an African-American widow with eight children. She was employed as a private cook. The census lists George as a widower, even though Lizzie still lived. He worked as a laborer in the cotton trade. Thompson Street was located in the vicinity of the rebuilding efforts on Forest Street near Spartan Mills and was very close to the Southern Railway Depot at Union Station. During this time, George may have worked loading and unloading cotton in the freight yard.

Carrie and Lizzie were kin. Lizzie's death certificate says that her parents were Carrie Shelton and Jake Gilliam. The 1870 federal census places this couple in the Jacks Township of Laurens County with three children, including an 8-year-old daughter listed as "Aree." The census taker probably misheard the child's name. By 1880, Jake and his 18-year-old daughter, listed correctly now as Carrie, had moved in with Shelton relatives in the Cross Keys community of Union County. Although Lizzie as a child has proven elusive, her connection to Carrie is undeniable.

Carrie's three youngest children, as of the 1910 census, were born around the time of and after the Pacolet flood. They were listed in this census out of chronological order as Dupre, 7; George, 1; and Booker, 4. Obviously, the name George raises questions.

Booker's death 32 years later provides two interesting clues. The informant on his death certificate was Iola Gilliam. She listed his father's name as George Castleberry, providing an alternate explanation for little George Gillam's paternity and name.

The 1911 Spartanburg city directory listed Trotting Sally as living at 121 Thompson Street — just two doors down from Carrie's original address. She was not listed in the directory. His occupation was documented as carpenter. He was no doubt working as a laborer at various construction sites in the city.

Spartanburg was growing at a rapid pace. Construction workers stayed busy adding to the town's mercantile core. George worked at the construction site of the Gresham Hotel, later renamed the Morgan Hotel. It was built in 1910 at the corner of Magnolia and West Charles streets just one block from Union Station. After years of neglect, the seven-story structure was demolished in June 1986. To commemorate the hotel's history, the Spartanburg Herald-Journal featured a number of local articles on the long-closed business. Several local residents were interviewed. Willard Thompson, who was 9 years old at the time of the construction, remembered seeing Trotting Sally working on the site. Thompson would watch the daily progress as he walked to school along Magnolia Street each morning. He recalled seeing "the well-known Spartanburg troubadour" pushing a wheelbarrow at the construction site.

One tale told in his obituary claims that Trotting Sally was involved in an accident at the Gresham construction site. He was hauling bricks in a wheelbarrow when "he got too brisk a start … and knocked another negro off the roof before he was able to stop." Neither of the main local newspapers reported the incident at the time. Perhaps he knocked the man from the scaffold close to the ground and the story simply was embellished over the years. It is interesting that this story resembles the one in Pacolet of Trotting Sally falling off a scaffold.

George didn't always work in Spartanburg. He also made frequent trips to Hendersonville, North Carolina, as early as 1912. Some North Carolina natives fondly remember hand-me-down stories of the man called Trotting Sally "who would walk the railroad tracks (at night) carrying two lanterns talking to himself." This could have been a trick to make it appear that he wasn't alone. Walking the rails alone was very risky — especially at night. They also remember that he would trot the streets of Hendersonville with his fiddle in a dirty flour sack. Sometimes he'd "throw his head up and down; chomp as on a bit as a high-spirited saddle horse does ... [and] neigh in [such] a realistic manner that horses would answer him." He also worked on various construction sites around Hendersonville.

Sally King Case, a native of Henderson County, was born in 1906 and remembered Mullins as a good friend of her father's. She recalled stories of the Spartanburg man trotting from Hendersonville to Greenville, South Carolina, "sometimes even beating the train." She also described "peering over the side of a wagon as a small girl watching this energetic black man." Case's father, George Washington Case, was accidentally shot in 1913 and died of complications from the wound. Giving Sally Case's age and the date of the death of her father, it appears that Trotting Sally was in Hendersonville about 1912-13. Other eyewitness and written accounts suggest he continued his trips to Hendersonville well into the 1920s.

Labor opportunities probably drew Trotting Sally to Hendersonville. Since train travel had been established in 1879, the little mountain town had grown steadily. Farm hands were needed, and construction jobs were available. Trotting Sally had free range after 1900. He accepted little responsibility and had a taste for adventure. He also may have realized the bonus of escaping the heat and high humidity of the South Carolina upcountry in the summer for the more tolerable climate of Hendersonville.

During this time, Lizzie lived in Campobello. She was a tenant farmer and, like George, claimed to be widowed. When asked, she would say she only had four children. At the time, Charlie was 30 years old and had moved out on his own. Barney, Ed and Matthew still lived at home with Lizzie. The fates of Riller and Richard are unknown. Why she failed to count them among her children is unclear.

George's name had never been recorded with a middle initial or name. Yet in the 1920 federal census he is listed as George W. Mullins, and his death certificate recorded his full name as George Washington Mullins. This suggests that he may have adopted his middle name from Sally Case's father. If so, he must have had a close friendship with Case to take his name.

11

In 1914, Archduke Franz Ferdinand of Austria, heir to the Austro-Hungarian throne, was assassinated. This unleashed a domino effect of European nations declaring war against each other. Three years later, on April 6, 1917, the United States declared war on Germany.

Spartanburg played a very important role in the war effort. On June 21, 1917, the U.S. War Department announced that Spartanburg would be one of 16 National Guard training camps to be constructed across the country. The city of Spartanburg leased about 2,000 acres three miles west of town to the U.S. government to build a camp called Wadsworth. Construction began and by the fall, troops began to arrive.

Fiske-Carter Construction Company was awarded the government contract to construct camp buildings on the site. Miles of water, power and sewer lines were laid by other contractors. New roads were paved. Local men were hired to do much of the labor. Any able-bodied man, white or black, could get work in short order. Although it is not certain whether George ever worked on any phase of the camp's construction, he was in the area at the time.

In September and October, nearly 30,000 men from New York arrived by train and began a vigorous eight-week training program. During this time, a short article in the Herald caught the attention of many locals. Its headline read, "Crazy Old Negro Got Soldiers' Goat." The article jokingly made light of a group of North Carolina Guardsmen. It stated that Trotting Sally was at the Union Station, pawing the ground and neighing at vehicles passing by. The Guardsmen decided to have a little fun. One took him by the arm saying, "Come on old horse, let's go to the stable." Sally "snapped viciously" and even showed signs of trying to bite. It was then that the soldiers decided "they needed reinforcements." Soon a dozen or more were seen running to help. The Herald reported that Sally "decided to be a squirrel, and scampered up a telephone pole." The young men tried to get him to come down, but he refused. It was then that one of the soldiers decided to climb up after him. The Herald went on to say that "Trotting Sally became a bird and soared over the heads of the ring of men." They started in pursuit, but "they didn't have wings and were soon left behind," concluding that "the soldiers spent the rest of the afternoon walking around in circles and staring at each other. Trotting Sally had got their goat and gone off with it."

George was 61 years old, which makes this account even more amazing. He was able to outwit and outperform these strapping young soldiers without causing harm to himself or others. Another story claims he actually climbed over the man who ascended the pole, which would have been an acrobatic move for any age, not to mention quite embarrassing for the soldiers.

Though Trotting Sally amused himself and many Spartans that day, doubtless he was quite aware that the war was no laughing matter. Three of his sons – Charlie, Barney and Ed

– had to face the draft boards. Barney was drafted and served first in the 156th Depot Brigade and later in Company D of the 339th Service Battalion. He was a private and served overseas for 10 months before being honorably discharged.

.

12

It is possible that Trotting Sally began playing fiddle as early as childhood. A 1907 New York Times article about him reported that "the violin also plays an important part in (his) everyday life," and that "he is never seen without his fiddle and bow strapped across his back; ... at the dinner hour he eats, jumps and plays." The article seems to imply that Mullins was a good and experienced fiddler.

An article in the Spartanburg Herald by Charles O. Hearon seems to date his fiddling to the early 1890s. Hearon was the author of a popular human interest column called "Hearon's Up Country." In the 1942 article, he responded to a postcard sent to him that inquired about Trotting Sally.

"For my correspondent's information "Trotting Sally" died a few years ago. Not many months ago, a son of Trotting Sally came in to pay his respects, saying at the time he lived on Mr. Traxler's Farm, not far from Rainbow Lake Road.... He said Trotting Sally just put on that act, at home he behaved just like other folks, though he did play his fiddle on all occasions."

In all likelihood, the son mentioned was Charlie, who lived near Rainbow Lake Road. Charlie was born about 1882, while Barney was born about 1894 and may have had little contact with his father. Considering their ages, one of the older sons may have been recalling a memory from childhood, thus dating his fiddling as early as 1890. However, it also is possible that the son may have simply recalled how his father acted years later.

Considering his skill level, though — dancing while playing and sawing words out on the strings — along with the fact that by 1907 the fiddle was seen as an extension of the man, it would be safe to assume that he began playing prior to 1890 if not much sooner. It is conceivable that he may have started fiddling in the years shortly after the Civil War. Fiddles, banjos, drums, and rhythm sticks, as well as other instruments, had been favorites in the region since the mid-1700s. Musicians — black and white, free and slave — were common figures at corn shuckings, frolics, weddings and other social gatherings. In some rare cases, white and black people even played together. Banjo playing also had become very popular, yet gradually began to decline in the African-American community in the latter half of the 19th century, due in part to the negative stereotypes associated with minstrel shows.

Trotting Sally no doubt observed the occasional street performer or medicine show act. When the circus came to town he made sure that he saw the shows, especially the musicians. These shows obviously had a profound influence on him, which echoed in his street acts. Mullins would swank out words on the strings, as any 19th-century street performer or medicine-show man might do, and add his own twist: cavorting about, barking and neighing. He probably incorporated a few popular tunes of the day into his act. He may have fiddled songs like "Bile Them Cabbages Down" or "Love Somebody" — tunes that came primarily from white musicians. His playlist may have included songs like "It Ain't Gonna Rain No More," sometimes called "A Little Snow, A Little Rain;" "Old Corn Licker" or "Pumpkin Pie," which were common banjo and fiddle tunes from African-American songsters of the Piedmont sections of South Carolina and North Carolina. He even could have performed popular minstrel/dance songs like "Arkansas Traveler" or "Mississippi Sawyer."

.

13

At 70 years old, George had experienced much in his life. As a child, he suffered the cruelty of human bondage and celebrated the jubilations of freedom. As a young man, he toiled many years in cotton fields as a sharecropper, tenant farmer and hired laborer. He loaded and unloaded freight cars, worked in the rail yard, dug ditches and worked as a construction laborer. He had married and fathered children. He had witnessed firsthand the face of discrimination, poverty and humiliation as he traveled throughout the region, including parts of North Carolina.

Racial tension was high in America in the early part of the 20th century. For most African Americans, very few changes of significance had taken place since emancipation. Many continued to live in poverty and lacked opportunity for education and new work skills. Jim Crow laws enforced segregation, second-class citizenship and corruption. These laws created obstacles to voting by African Americans, Native Americans and other non-whites, and few held office.

Spartanburg was recognized at this time as a growing little town with a bright future. Textile manufacturing in this railroad hub was the primary reason for this growth. Since the turn of the century, thousands of people migrated to the area in search of work in mills. By the 1920s, the county was scattered with cotton-mill villages. Downtown Spartanburg teemed with businesses that catered to the needs of the community. New schools, churches and a public hospital were built. Spartanburg had its own free library. Many residences gained indoor plumbing and electricity.

The African-American population also had grown. Communities dotted the countryside. Most were loosely connected "tenant" communities woven together by agriculture — mostly cotton production. Some of these communities had their own schools and churches. There were other communities that were more structured and independent, with few wants or needs from white people — communities like Little Africa in northern Spartanburg County and Happy Land in Greenville County. Spartanburg's South Side had a high black population, along with African-American schools, churches, shops, barbershops and grocery and hardware stores. This community south of Main Street was in part self sustaining, with its own social and economic infrastructure.

On July 4, 1911, a short article appeared in the Spartanburg Herald. The headline read, "Trotting Sally's Son Gets the First Marriage License." The newspaper reported, "The first license issued in Spartanburg County went to Charles Ernest Mullen, a negro, the son of 'Trotting Sally' — so called because of his delusion that he is a horse." The article said that Charles paid a $1.00 fee, and that he gave his age as 29 years old. Also mentioned was his fiancée, 24-year-old Leila White. The report concluded, "Both live on the place of Mr. Cicero Wolfe, at Brannon, near Boiling Springs." Wolfe was a white landowner and farmer. Charlie may have been a sharecropper on Wolfe's farm.

In 1920 Charlie was tenant farming, living in the vicinity of Little Africa on Mills Gap Road, now S.C. Highway 9, north of New Prospect. He and Leila or Lela had three young sons – John Henry, Roy Lee and Bennie Bee – and a daughter, Mattie Lee. The federal census of that year also revealed that Charlie's father, George, lived with them. It said he was 64 years old, a farm laborer and widowed.

Charlie's younger brother, Barney, lived nearby on Plantation Road, which was located near Campobello. Barney and his wife, Ellen, had one child, 6-year-old Ruth. Lizzie Mullins, still alive despite George's claims, also lived in the household. Her age was recorded as 48. Like her estranged husband, she also claimed to be widowed.

The census was conducted in mid-February 1920. That winter was harsh, with the temperature in the county the previous month reported at a low of 7 degrees. George probably stayed with Charlie and family, waiting for the spring thaw. Charlie was a proud man, religious in character, who almost always wore a suit and tie with shined shoes. He may have taken after his grandfather, Samuel, and provided a structured environment and safety net for his father to fall back on. Barney may have provided the same for their mother. It is not clear whether George and Lizzie still communicated. They may have kept up with each other through family conversation. They probably considered themselves divorced in a state that did not legalize the dissolution of marriage until 1949.

The popular belief is that Trotting Sally was rootless, wandering aimlessly from place to place. This is far from the truth. He was more methodical in his travels, planning his stays with people he knew and calculating seasons, weather and events. To a degree he followed the work. He spent most of spring and fall in Spartanburg or the vicinity, and during the hot summer he traveled to North Carolina. During the harsh winter months, George simply hibernated with family. While in Spartanburg he rented a room or stayed with someone he knew. He frequented the African-American section of town south of Main. He also likely spent a great deal of time on Short Wofford Street, where renowned black street musicians such as Pink Anderson and Blind Simmie Dooley often played. He always had a place to hang his battered hat and fiddle.

During his frequent winter stays with Charlie, George probably helped his son with household and farm chores. He may have hired himself out to neighboring farmers as well. When springtime rolled around, he became restless. With fiddle and bow on his back, hat turned up, and a big smile on his face, Trotting Sally left. He would trot into town, play a little on the streets, find a construction job and stay a while. He would visit other areas in the region, all the while performing on the streets and working odd jobs.

George was an opportunist, taking advantage of his environment as well as other factors. He went where work was plentiful. Local contractors and farmers considered him to be a fine laborer. He would work a week or so and then play for tips on the streets for a few days, returning to the construction site and repeating the process over and over. When the circus or fair was in town, he made sure that he was free and could play for tips. When the train station was active with travelers, he made sure he was within earshot as they dined at local establishments or visited shops. Sometimes he simply would create his own show on the sidewalk or street corner, drawing people to see him dance and play his fiddle.

14

Trotting Sally was aware that he was a colorful character and exaggerated that aspect of his personality accordingly, but his natural energetic awkwardness combined with his reclusive tendencies helped to define his legendary persona. Locals love to tell how he could outrun trains and automobiles and work twice as long and hard without tiring. He seemed to be everywhere, obvious to locals as they passed him on the street. He always lightly trotted, which has been described as a kind of half run, half trot, with an occasional dart or forward leap. He sometimes trotted around in circles and kicked — all the while playing his fiddle, snapping and neighing. To some he appeared skittish or easy to frighten. A simple glimpse of Trotting Sally occasionally would begin a conversation about his supernatural abilities. Each local storyteller no doubt added a little to the tale as if they had actually witnessed the events themselves. In rare cases when someone would ask Trotting Sally about his abilities, he would paw at the ground and howl and then take off running. These were no doubt actions that fueled many of the stories.

Perhaps the most popular story that locals told is that he could outrace horses, buggies and automobiles. One story even has him beating a Model T from Pacolet to Spartanburg.

There also are numerous tales of him racing trains. Such stories have him outrunning the trains that ran to Spartanburg from Cowpens, Inman and Chesnee. Some of these stories place him after the race sitting at the next rail station waiting for the train to pull in.

Countless stories have been retold about different races and locations. Though these tales seem impossible they may have originated with one event, with the rest being more folktale than fact. The origin of Trotting Sally outrunning trains may have stemmed from a story told of him racing a train that ran from Lyman to Wellford. These towns — about a mile apart — are located close to where he lived as a young man in Beech Springs. Wellford was a bustling little community that had a post office, general store and train depot. Lyman, a newer community, was originally called Groce Stop. It was named for Augustus Belton Groce, who ran a general store beside the railroad tracks. Groce Stop was no more than a flagged stop then. The train would have had a scheduled stop at the Wellford station. Considering the distance, Trotting Sally could have outrun a slow starting and stopping locomotive between these stops, thus creating the origin of the legendary tale.

A strange twist to this tale is that it says he outran the Piedmont & Northern — an electric passenger train established in 1914. If so, he would have been almost 60 years old at the time. Yet considering his energy and athletic spirit, it should not be discounted.

Another very popular legend relates how he raced a train from Fairforest to Spartanburg. He handed the conductor his hat while at the Fairforest depot then took off running, only to be waiting at the next station when the train pulled in to get his hat back. The P&N's depot was west of Spartanburg at Clevedale, where Fairforest Finishing was established in 1929, and not as far west as the Fairforest community itself. At a distance of about 4.5 miles as the crow flies, the sprint would not have been impossible for a practiced runner.

Though the public saw Trotting Sally as a solo act, one story suggests that he may have briefly had an assistant. Legend has it that he used a small boy named Jabo to collect tips for him during his street performances. It is said that Jabo would ride on Trotting Sally's back with his feet in his back pockets. While Trotting Sally busked, the little boy wondered in and out of the crowd with a hat or cup collecting money from onlookers.

Jabo's identity remains a mystery, but one possible scenario is that he was one of Carrie's children. If George left Pacolet for Spartanburg sometime after 1900 and moved in with her, he would have had regular contact with her young children. One of her children, Jacob, was born about 1898. The names Jacob and Jabo are similar, yet a link cannot be established.

Carrie had four sons who were small children during the first decade of the 20th century. There could have been a progression of nephews who accompanied Trotting Sally who, to the public eye or in later retellings, all blended into a single child called Jabo.

Several stories briefly mention that George liked to fish and hunt. These activities were necessary for poor people during this time. Many Spartans north of town had their own fishing spots along the creeks and streams of the Lawson's Fork, Shoally and Chinquapin. Mullins may have frequented a spot at the filtration plant reservoir, where present-day highways 221 and 9 intersect, which was a popular fishing spot north of town. He may have hunted for small game, setting out rabbit-gums and traps hidden in the brushes and along the creeks. A shiny 5-cent piece would get him a handful of potatoes and carrots; add an onion and he had the makings of a fine rabbit stew.

In street performances, Trotting Sally would tell people that he made his fiddle and her name was Rosalie. In all likelihood, he did not make the fiddle featured in the famous photograph by Alfred T. Willis. It appears to be an inexpensive model that was commonly sold at general stores and mercantile shops. Rosalie was always with him, a staple of his street shows. Sometimes he would talk to her as he played. "Rosalie, you hungry?" he would ask. Then he'd take his fiddle-bow and scratch it across the strings to make it sound like, "Y-E-S." He then would ask, "What you want to eat?" Then he would scratch out, "P-E-A-C-H P-I-E." Other times he would engage the crowd in his short scripts with Rosalie. He'd say, "Look at that pretty girl. What color is her dress?" He then would make the violin swank, "R-E-D." That was a real crowd pleaser.

Some stories were nothing more than tall tales. There is a rare story of him tossing a brick over the Montgomery Building. In its day, the Montgomery Building was a fine accomplishment for the city of Spartanburg and would be for many years. Built in 1928, its 10 stories housed office and retail space and a theater. Tossing a brick over the building would have been an impossible feat for anyone, not to mention a 72-year-old man. Perhaps he worked on the construction site, and the tall tale surfaced years later.

George was always a welcome sight. Just one glimpse of the man "who thinks he is a horse" never failed to amuse. A local might announce that he saw Trotting Sally a few miles down the road heading to town. When he arrived he might stop and play part of a tune on his fiddle, howl or bark. He always drew a crowd as he danced and talked to his fiddle. Adults would introduce him to a new generation, saying "Look! There's Trotting Sally!" To many, he seemed a timeless soul.

Trotting Sally frequented the Inman area as well. He likely passed through as early as 1910, while on his way to Hendersonville. In the 1920s, he lived and worked in the area for a brief time. In fact, George worked on the Inman Mills construction site in 1928.

Many Inman residents recalled seeing him at the town's train depot. One remembered him leaning against a power pole near the depot downtown playing his fiddle. During the 1920s, there were at least two passenger trains that stopped in Inman. O.B. Henderson, a long-time Inman Mills resident, recalled that as a child he would sometimes stay up late at night and listen to him play his fiddle.

Inman residents also tell a story about him picking cotton on a local farm. It is said that Trotting Sally always would carry his fiddle strapped to his back, even while he was in the field. When he would finish picking a row — always well ahead of others — he would stop to play his fiddle. Another story claims that sometimes he would hide in the bushes along the roadside. When an unsuspecting motorist would come down the road, Trotting Sally would leap out in a playful manner, begin playing his fiddle, start barking and running beside the automobile. Others recalled that he would stand in the middle of the street and make his fiddle "talk" for the children. When they got a little too close he would bark and they would fall back, only to inch closer once more. Many children loved to see Trotting Sally but he frightened some, especially the older youths who would hang back from the strange man.

15

George's wife, Lizzie, told the federal census taker on June 21, 1900, that she was born in August 1869. She almost certainly shaved a few years off her actual age and probably was born around the year the Civil War ended in 1865. The practice continued throughout each census in which she participated, with her age changing as little as five years and as many as 13 in the decade spans.

Lizzie must have been a strong-willed woman. She worked hard to take care of her children and husband while she farmed, cooked and cleaned. George counted on Lizzie to keep them going, even though he was not always dependable and sometimes was gone or busy doing what he wanted to do. For at least a dozen years through hard work, disappointments, struggles and poverty, Lizzie was able to keep the family together.

After George deserted her in the early 1900s, Lizzie carried on as best as she could. Prior to 1910, she moved with her children to the Campobello area. She was the head of the household and a tenant farmer. The younger children were old enough to help out. Sometime before 1920, she moved in with Barney and his family. Barney was able to provide for her well enough that she no longer had to toil in the fields, and her health may have begun to deteriorate.

On December 15, 1923, Lizzie died. The cause of death was uterine cancer. The death certificate indicates that she had not been under medical care long, perhaps as little as three weeks. Barney provided information about her parents, Jake and Carrie Shelton Gilliam. She was buried on December 26. The place of burial was not recorded on the death certificate.

16

By 1930, George was staying part of the time in an area just north of Boiling Springs in the vicinity of the Mud Creek community. Charlie's oldest son, John Henry Mullins, also lived in the area.

The countryside was rural farmland, inhabited by African-American tenant families. Ridgeville Baptist Church, commonly pronounced as Reidville or Reidsville, served the community as a school and place of worship. The church is located off Zimmerman Lake Road on Ridgeville Baptist Church Road. Charlie, John Henry and their families were active members of the church. John Henry's children attended grade school there, and both Charlie and John Henry are buried in the cemetery. George may have attended services there as well.

In the summer of 1931, George turned 75 years old. He was worn and tattered. He had spent all of his life working very hard, exposed to the elements and the everyday dangers of farm and construction work. His spirit had been strong and always waxing. He never seemed to tire. But in the summer of 1931, he became ill. He was weak with fever and suffered frequent bouts of nausea. His symptoms continued to worsen, and his cheerful spirit began to wane. He took to bed, but the pain he felt deep in his stomach did not go away. His eyes and skin yellowed as his symptoms worsened. A physician began seeing him on September 11 and told him his liver had gone bad. Perhaps he gave him morphine for the pain. On Sunday, September 20, 1931, George Washington Mullins passed away. He was alone. Charlie discovered his father's body the next day.

Because of the common mispronunciation of the church's name, the newspaper and death certificate listed his place of burial as Reidville Baptist Church. But it was at Ridgeville Baptist Church, on Sunday, September 27th at 2 p.m., that George was laid to rest. Woodward Funeral Home was the undertaker. The weather was pleasant. The grave simply was marked with a fieldstone. It is likely that most of the congregation attended the service, along with family, friends and a few curious onlookers. Some white people may have paid their respects as well.

Just what the preacher said at the funeral service is unknown, but it was the African-American community that knew George best. To many he was a brother, born in the crib of slavery — the first generation of free men and the last to know what it meant to be enslaved. Surviving the earthly confines of segregation and the Jim Crow laws that held him down, at last he truly was a free man with no rules to control his tongue, break his spirit or turn him away. He had entered the Promised Land with his father and mother, where he could dance and sing and play his fiddle.

Few newspaper articles reported positive events about African Americans during this time. It was rare to have an obituary. The Spartanburg Herald gave him a headline, a subhead and eight paragraphs at the top of the page. It celebrated the life of the "well known and eccentric figure" and made sure that people knew him not just as Trotting Sally, but as George Mullins.

For some, there must have been a feeling of sadness to lose such a storied character. For many years, he had been a part of the community with his loping gait and music. While few understood him, many embraced him. His was the sort of passing by which people marked time. Locals continued to share the many stories of Trotting Sally outrunning trains, playing a tune on Rosalie and trotting along dusty roads. He was gone, but to this day not forgotten.

George's death was diagnosed as "malignancy of the liver, probably involving his esophagus." Though the cause of liver cancer is not always known, certain hepatitis infections and alcoholic cirrhosis are two that often are seen. During the Prohibition era of the 1920s, illegal alcohol was not always safe to consume. Over a period of time, he may have damaged his liver consuming moonshine.

On the other hand, considering his age and vitality it is unlikely that alcohol was a major factor. There are no stories of him ever being drunk or acting drunk, which would imply that if he did take a sip from time to time, it was not much. Yet consuming even small amounts of tainted homemade spirits over a long period could have played a factor.

17

The legend of Trotting Sally would have been no more than a collection of fading stories about an odd old black man if it were not for Willis, the enterprising Spartanburg photographer. The Williston native moved to Spartanburg in 1912 and got a job developing and printing Kodak film at Ligon's Drug Store downtown. Willis wanted to be behind the camera though, and eventually moved into a career in commercial photography.

Willis helped capture on film life in Spartanburg during the Great Depression. He would lug his cumbersome equipment around town to document both everyday and important events. He created an impressive photo collection, now archived at the Spartanburg County Public Libraries.

Sometime in 1923 on a clear day, Willis made the only known photograph of Trotting Sally. The legendary photograph, which was taken in front of a store, captures George sitting with his fiddle tucked under his chin, bow in hand resting gently on the strings. On his head rests a turned-up hat. His clothes are tattered, patched and mended. Flanked to his left are well buckets and salt licks. Behind him are stacked boxes and a steel curtain. Mullins poses for the camera, motionless, with a proud look of accomplishment. He appears almost justified and content, as if he had been planning this picture for a lifetime. He probably never viewed the photograph.

Willis loved to experiment with new technology. By the late 1920s, he was tinkering with the silent black-and-white moving pictures of the day. He wasted no time in filming historical events, such as Charles Lindbergh's flight over Spartanburg in October 1927. He also filmed politicians such as James F. Byrnes, as well as parades, speeches and even cockfights.

Willis also filmed Spartanburg's most unique personality, Trotting Sally. The film clip, which is about 30 seconds long, appears to show him performing at two locations. It is not clear whether the events were staged or impromptu, though it would have taken Willis a little time to set up and focus the camera. One segment appears to show Trotting Sally in a street performance, the other at a construction site. Trotting Sally seems to play solely for the camera on the street and is certainly aware of it in the construction scene. In the latter, he performs before a small crowd of African-American men. In action that belies his 71 years, he fiddles and dances, shows off and smiles. The short segment ends with him quickly stopping, turning his head and howling or barking.

The silent filmstrip underscores several important facts. His fiddling appears to be exceptionally skillful. He comes across as a polished craftsman with a flair for entertainment. The rare piece also shows him with a guitar swinging from his back as he dances and fiddles away — the first and only evidence to suggest that he played other instruments. In fact, no known stories exist that speak of him playing or owning other instruments. Considering his age, Trotting Sally seems to possess the agility and spirit of a man much younger. Perhaps the most important observation is that he looks normal and very much in control, which in itself answers many questions about his personality and mental stability.

18

At the time of Trotting Sally's death, the Great Depression was crippling the United States. A world war would follow. Despite the fact that the news of his passing was reported in the Herald, many did not know of it. Sightings continued to surface of the "crazy old Negro" who thought he was a horse. These sightings simply were mistaken identities fueled by legend.

Over the years, locals continued to retell the stories. Some details and descriptions changed with the telling. Many have wondered what happened to his fiddle, Rosalie. None of the folktales and legends tells of the whereabouts of it. Many assumed he was buried with it, or one of his family members had it tucked away somewhere.

The fact is after his death Trotting Sally's few belongings, including his fiddle, were claimed by his grandson, John Henry Mullins. The fiddle was stored in a dresser drawer. A few years after George's death, John Henry's young children discovered it. They snuck it out and played with it, eventually destroying it. The pieces were discarded. Any other belongings soon were forgotten and lost.

Folktales are the only mementos of George's life. Locals still mention him as the man who would outrun trains, bark like a dog and play his fiddle at a drop of a hat. These wonderful stories live on as simple hand-me-down tales of another time and place. Spartanburg has changed, yet some things remain the same. Memories fade and people forget, yet treasures remain. George Mullins was a treasure, a legend that will live on forever.

ABOUT THE AUTHOR

For more than 30 years, John Thomas Fowler has worked to preserve the traditions and stories of yesteryear. John has been a contributing writer for various publications concerning old-time music and musicians. He also has produced several distinctive popular recordings of traditional/roots and ethnic musicians and storytellers.

Recently John served as the state scholar for the Smithsonian exhibit project "New Harmonies: Celebrating American Roots Music" and continues to serve as a scholar in The Humanities Council South Carolina's Speakers Bureau.

John's many years of dedication to South Carolina history was recognized by the South Carolina General Assembly in May 2013, when they presented him with the Jean Laney Harris Folk Heritage Award.

John grew up in the upcountry of South Carolina, where he still resides. He is a graduate of the Institute for Community Scholars, Folklore & Music Studies at Swannanoa College. He is a founding member of the Carolina Old Time Music Network and co-produces a very popular old-time music show, "This Old Porch," on North Carolina public radio WNCW 88.7.

Visit www.hairytoeproductions.com to learn more about John Thomas Fowler.

Andy Brooks, fiddler:

"John has spent much of his life preserving and sharing the folk heritage of South Carolina. He is a highly respected and admired ambassador of tradition. Celebrating and sharing our heritage is not merely a facet of John's life, it is the life in which he lives every day."

H. Dean Watson, Pickens County Cultural Commission:

"He [John] has worked tirelessly and creatively to preserve folk music, folk music performers, storytelling, and folk craftsmanship for our state [South Carolina]."

Randy L. Akers, executive director,
The Humanities Council South Carolina:

"John Fowler is an excellent historian, a strong speaker and performer, and a passionate advocate for the importance of folk arts."

INDEX